uh-oh

poems

David Gregory Young

Wild at Art Publishing

uh-oh
poems
by David Gregory Young

Copyright 2008 ©
by David Gregory Young

All rights reserved. No part of this book may be reproduced or transmitted in any form or by any means, electronic or mechanical, including photocopying, recording, or by an information storage and retrieval system, without permission in writing from the Publisher.

Published by Wild at Art Publishing, 2053 NW 79th Ave, JBC SJO #16220, Miami, FL 33122, wild.at.art@hotmail.com, (866) 669-6798

International Standard Book Number: 978-0-615-25485-2

Cover design and art by David Gregory Young

for my princess, Sibel

read this slow

i

wrote it slow

i think
        too much
                i think

the light of
liberty
is a candle
that
burns in the
wind

dreams
    only
come true for
    those
who dare
    to dream

dare to dream

maybe we will
figure it all
out just in
time to be
too late

technology

today i saw the
last daffodil
it was no different
than any
of the other hundreds
thousands millions that
came before it
was just that it was the
last daffodil

last daffodil

aim for the stars

    if you fall short

you'll reach the sky

seems like i'm

    always going the

long way round

sometimes
i don't
 miss you
  any more
  and
 maybe somehow
  that's the
   saddest part
   of it
   all

sometimes i feel

like

a waste of space

there are things you have never

thought of

that you will never

think of

ever thought of that

all of life

is

infinite

variety

and

infinite

possibility

i used to have an
        inferiority complex
then i found out that
      i was inferior

you don't have to be right

to know something's wrong

late, i catch a scent
it is you but where?
heart quickens, a faint
smile, ahh ha! the
hand. fading fast, but
there surely as you
were.

i'm a creature of
        the garden
    and
i want to go home

intricately deceived

every day

    is beautiful

        in its

            own unique

            way

alone am i
and
don't know why
alone am i
and
want to cry
alone am i
and
could just die
alone am i
and
instead sigh
alone am i

there is a
        tribe of
                stone age
                      indians in
            Brazil
who count
        only to the
number two anything
        more than that
        is called many
and we think
                we're
                  advanced

freedom is always

bought with blood

ours

we erred

when

we feared

the
    tree said you'll
      be sorry
   and after some thought
   i realized the tree was
right so i didn't cut
       down
   the
     tree

no matter how hard
you squeeze a
pillow
it won't hug back

if you pray for rain

carry an umbrella

stop tearing down
        spider webs

start
        observing them

who will i find

if i

lose myself in you

the real blind
　people in this
　　　world are not
　　　　　those who can not
　　　　　　　see
but
　those
　　who
　　　refuse
　　　　to
　　　　　see

the grass is always
greener on the other
    side of the fence
but it
        still turns brown
in the winter

i wanna be a tree

then i could have
roots
and still leave

how quickly the time has gone
that once promised to be so
long

life

the system's a friend
      of those within
but what about
      those without

invariably infinite

very little have i
  very little need i
      everything have i
           and more
be rid of this
     and have more
be rid of that
     and have more
be rid of everything
     and have all
  in everything
      is nothing
  in nothing
      is everything

i want to touch you
but i'm afraid you'll burn me like a white hot fire
i want to smell you
but i'm afraid you'll quicken an intense desire
i want to see you
but i'm afraid you'll grow more beautiful on sight
i want to hear you
but i'm afraid you'll strike a chord of pure delight
i want to taste you
but i'm afraid you'll send me into a frenzy
of
love

passersby
briskly
    to and fro
        do they see
            me
       am i here
no eye contact
          forbidden
    too
    intimate
      why
so cold
       look at
        me
i'm drowning in
      a
    sea of
       indifference

your
    dancing
  is
    so
       beautiful

i can hardly
  watch it
    but i
      still see
        your
          dancing

i rode by
      this used car lot
with
    a sign that said
        no credit
            bad credit
        no problem
i rode by
    some time later
    and it was
      empty
i guess it
    was
     a
        problem

chance favors the prepared mind *

the
ultimate
harbinger
of destiny
is
love

if
      you
  give
      till
    it
hurts
    it
   starts

      to
         feel
    good

when

Van Gogh

was living

he

couldn't give away

his

paintings   &

now

you

can't

buy

one

so

who

was

confused

some
folks
have
more
dollars
than
sense

when
i   was
         six
  my great grandpa
      sat
    me on
           his knee
       and
          told me
             that
       all a man
            needs
 in this life
          is
 a
   good
        woman
        a
           good
              horse
 and
    a good
    dog
         but not
       necessarily
in
  that order

be
here
now

yesterday
      is a
          memory
tomorrow
      is a
        dream
today
      is

today is

at last
  there
      was
just
    the
       sound
   of
  the ocean
       &
        the
     cicadas

       &

then   just

      the

          ocean
       &
       then

```
he said
there's
        dolphin
    & pelicans
            off
        the
    point &
        she
            said
                thanks
        i
            needed

            that
```

by
    sunset
        you
could
  not
    tell
where
the sea
&
  the
sky met
&
then
i
  knew
they
were
one

please
　　　　don't
　learn
　　　　how
not
　　　　to
　　　　　　cry

the
    moon
  is
       smiling
 a
   star
      is winking
   the
       heavens
           are
      singing
            your
                name

living

simply

      is

   very

complex

worlds
    collide
soon
      i
  dare

i
         no
think
              right
      lately

deep down we are all the same

where
    have
i been
    all
    my
        life

truth
 be told
    common
sense
      is
 not
     so
 common

that's
your
         problem
         he said
stop
     thinking
       so
          much
   &
    start
        feeling

the
    wind
blows
    where
it
    will

dreams
     change

this
    would
  be
   the
     most
beautiful
    life
       if
  we could
   just
     get
 over
    how
  impossible
it
  all   seems

```
it    was so
    small   and
barely green
        enough not
                to be
        dead
            &
        there
            was
        a palm
            tree

            inside
```

i was
　　in a
dugout canoe
　　　on　a
　　remote river estuary
with
　　an older
　　　man native
　　　　to
　the area
　　　who told
　　me
　　　how
crystal clear the
　　　water

　　　　used
　　　　 to
　　　　 be

all
     my
life
     might
have
     been *

assume
the
extreme

never
assume
the
extreme

infinite
compassion

rule
your
    temper

sometimes
to
find
your
way
you
have
to
get
lost

when
 i
was a
child
 i
thought
 i
knew it all
now
 i
know
 i
was
  right

the
two

hardest
words
to say
are i'm
sorry & the three
easiest
are
i
love
you

    &   then
                    she

escaped
                back

    to her

        cell

if
      your
           prince
     turns
        out
          to
        be
a
    frog
         at
least   he
         might
    croak
        soon

if
       you
              love

       you
              risk

great
          loss

  if
         you

                never
     love
           you
              never

       live

everything

      fades   away

slowly into

                yesterday

     nothing here

is   here   to

      stay

         everything

fades

     away

fades away

if i didn't

have u

wouldn't know what

to do

& i would be so

blue if i didn't have

u

psycho – logically
speaking

what

do you do

when all your
dreams
have come true
&
still   you   wake

up

&

find your self

blue

if
you
look
in
the
rear-view mirror
too often
you might
just run
off the
road

```
        now
i
        see
                the
past
                clearly

                &
        thinking

straight
                hurts
```

&
then
he said
she
had
black hair
&
black eyes
&
a crystal
clear
heart

crystal clear heart

have

you

seen me

i lost

me

somewhere

love
  is
    the
      purest
      form
        of
          madness

sometimes
    we
say
    a lot
      when

we

  say

    nothing

```
how
    can
        i
    ever
        bear    this
                    sorrow


my  son
            was

                coming

            home

tomorrow



        last day in combat
```

can
    this all
be   just
    a
   fantasy
  or
   is

   reality
  my
    dream
     come
true

dream come true

&
then
he
said
she
was
beautiful
to
the
soul

beautiful to the soul

the
 evanescence
   is
dissipating
     &
i'm
  no
   longer

 afraid   of
    what's
     on
the
   other
     side

the other side

there
are
worse
things
than
dying
&
one
of
them
is
living
in

fear

living in fear

don't pack your
nuts away like
a squirrel
don't act
like it's not
the
end of
the world

end of the world

she
        said
i got
         engaged

     today
&

he
    said

congratulations
        as
  his
      heart sank
        like
      the

       titanic

&
she knew
the name
of every
flower
&
she knew
the
sound
of
every
bird
&
she
made
the   sunshine
brighter
that
day

stop

  dreaming

   &

 start

   scheming

&
then
her words
fell on
me
like
drops
of
dew

drops of dew

all
  truly
     great
art
    is
  born
   of
    pain

born of pain

i
    don't
talk
   to
people
     who
        don't
    talk
      to
   themselves
     but
   they need
    a
good
    talking to

irrelevance
　　is
　　the
　　　new
relevance

you
    are
        more
            beautiful
than sunshine
        &
    when the soft
wind whispers
        slowly it
speaks your name
      &
    i see you
      in
        my

dreams

if
      you
          believe
            in
everything
              you
   don't
         believe
      in

    anything

many people
          go through life
    staring at the
            writing on the
wall
        &
     never realize that the
          pen was in their
              hand

love
&
reason
share
no
season

things
	have
		changed

* Louis Pasteur
* Sidney Carton "A Tale of Two Cities" Charles Dickens

David Gregory Young was born in Southeast Louisiana, and studied creative writing, geography and history at Louisiana State University. This is a collection of his favorite poems, collected for almost 20 years. They are quips, quotes and anecdotes that were born in the spirit of pure poetry. He currently resides in Costa Rica and spends his time writing and producing music, creating abstract paintings, and is always on the lookout for a great photograph.

••

This book is dedicated to my family who love me unconditionally despite my being a genuine lunatic.

www.ingramcontent.com/pod-product-compliance
Ingram Content Group UK Ltd.
Pitfield, Milton Keynes, MK11 3LW, UK
UKHW051254180426
11947UKWH00020B/1710